Jesus Read my Letters

Indra Watson

Presentation by *BookLeaf Publishing*

Web: www.bookleafpub.com

E-mail: info@bookleafpub.com

ISBN: 9789357619547

First edition 2022

DEDICATION

To my family, friends, teachers and Cathie R. and Cynthia F., who along the way have never stopped encouraging me to keep writing and aiming for my goals.

This book is also dedicated to the following churches located in upstate New York: Universal Baptist Church; New Life Fellowship Church; and Bridge Christian Church.

Last but never least, in loving memory of my grandmother Harriet, my beloved brother Gussy and my mommy Karen.

PREFACE

From a very young age, I used diaries to write letters
addressed to Jesus. I knew there was no better One to
tell precious secrets and misfortunes to. Besides
attending church with my grandmother as a child, I
can attribute my earliest memories of believing in
God to the movie Forest Gump: When Jenny prayed
for God to make her a bird. I resonated with her
character in some ways and the way that God
answered her prayer in the movie empowered me to
pray and trust in Him.

This book started out as a poetry writing challenge
and then it became so much more. I decided to make
my first book of poetry strictly about how faith in
God has shaped my life for the better. It is with
careful consideration that I have chosen to share
some of my more private experiences in a way that I
hope shows my respect for God while being
transparent about my shortcomings and spiritual
journey.

It is my hope that something within these pages
inspires even one person in this world to find, regain
or rediscover their own faith journey. At the very
least, I hope something within these works ignites
appreciation and celebration for your life. Even if the
reading of this book ends here, I am eternally
thankful.

Begin Anew

Where do I begin?
This is the chapter where I'm born again.
This time with real purpose and intent:
To live in Jesus means to be content.
I will rejoice no matter the trial or tribulation.
For the Good News is always cause for
celebration!

Jesus read my letter.
Now my life is all the better.
He heard my cries.
He helped me discern the truth from the lies.
He gave me a new direction.
He forgave me for all repented transgression.
He knows I am not perfect.
He just wants to know my heart is earnest.

Nearer Still

Draw near to me Lord, I need you.
Even in the darkness, I can feel you.
I know this is not the end.
For You Lord are a constant friend!

God, help me to let go.
Let Your Living Waters flow.
I can feel Jesus' blood cleanse my soul.
The Living Bread keeps me full.

I want to grow and wither not
Lord, please heal my heart.
I know You are letting things fall apart so other
things fall together.
I know whatever I give to You, You can make
better.

Thank You for finding some things in me worth
saving.
You can fill any parts of my flesh still craving.
I lift my hands when I can't lift my heavy heart.
Thank You for a fresh start.

I can feel your amazing grace breaking my
shackle.

There is nothing with Your protection I cannot
tackle.
I can feel the weightlessness of Your yoke.
I know that I am rich even when I am monetarily
broke.

Thank You for giving me immeasurable reasons
to shout Hallelujah!
Lord, I'll never stop having love for Ya.

A Dance with Jesus

Dance with me Jesus, across life's dance floor.
Help me learn the steps to overcome more.
Lift me in the air when obstacles keep me
stumbling.
Spin me 'round 'til my burdens start crumbling.
If I should miss a beat,
please place a lamp by my feet.
If I backslide in this dance,
please grant me another chance.
I trust that my steps You will order.
So will You do me this honor?
Hold me closer when the dance gets harder.
For in this dance of life You are the best partner!

Open Poem to the Broken

This is an open poem to the broken and the lost.
A reminder that there's Someone who loved you
enough to cover your sins' cost.
We can be grateful for this Good News.
We can sing praises at times we once sung the
blues.
This is what it feels like to live in liberation.
Freedom from the wages of sin is cause for
celebration.

When you're at rock bottom, there's only one
way to look - which is up.
He will meet you where you are and cover you
in love!
He will fill the crevices of your broken heart.
He can mend what has been torn apart!
He won't force His way inside if you don't want
Him to yet.
But if you receive Him, you will gain the best
peace yet.

This concludes my open poem to the depressed
and those who feel alone.
There's a Loving Father waiting to welcome you
home.

Salutation of the Seasons

I will dance for the Lord in the summertime.
Sand under my feet feels so fine.
Warm sun on my skin, counting shells I found.
Nature is where I feel God all around!

I will dance for the Lord in the autumnal breeze.
Cruising down the byways amongst colorful
leaves.
Breathtaking sunrises and sunsets painting the
top of my town.
Nature is where I feel God all around!

I will dance for the Lord in the springtime heat.
Admiring new flowers are such a treat!
I enjoy a soothing melodic bird sound.
Nature is where I feel God all around!

I will dance for the Lord in winter's chill.
For I know there's not an emptiness that God
can't fill.
I long one day to be with Him and in Heaven to
receive a crown.
Nature is where I feel God all around!

Winter, fall, summer and spring.
I know God has made everything.
So much beauty He created for us to see.
The Talented One who made all this nature made
you and me.

He made us to move, sent his Son to give us
another chance.
I will thank the Lord through song and dance!
I will dance for the Lord in all seasons.
I will dance for the Lord for all reasons.

Dear Heavenly Father, thank You for nature.
Thank You for insects and every creature.
Thank You for living things flying and on the
ground.
Thank You for Your presence all around!

Leaving her Legs and Legacy

Mommy could no longer use her legs.
But she never stopped giving God praise.

She prayed to Him on good days and days she
fell down.
She trusted God to help her reach higher ground.

She knew God was bigger than Multiple
Sclerosis.
She knew He'd get her through this.

I thank God for the faith she inspired me with.
It was a lot to see as a kid.

God blessed me with a caregiver heart.
God bound together what Satan meant to tear
apart.

The old adage says that a family stays together
that prays together.
Mommy saw rainbows no matter the weather.

God had given her in those short years all that
she had ever wanted.

She found courage to smile in moments others
would have grunted.

Dear God, give me a peace such as this.
Dear God, give me a joy such as this.

Mommy's legs stopped working for her when I
was eighteen.
But her faith remained steadfast through her last
breaths in 2018.

Loved Differently

Eros love came without knowing
and left faster than a whirlwind blowing.
I was not ready for it all.
I was not ready for the fall.
But it surely came.
A fire that I could not tame.

His darkness complimented mine.
His humor helped me leave the past behind.
And for a while I felt this was all I would need.
Then I cried until God each time he made my
heart bleed.
I kept waiting for it to be our time.
But he was never going to be just mine.

It took time to understand that love and
friendship can't be bought.
I learned to lean on Jesus, for there is spiritual
warfare to be fought.
At times I can't quell my ruminating.
I remind myself not to learn on my own
understanding.
At times holding thoughts captive leaves me
trembling.

Other times I can't help sharing it with others
with rambling.
That's when it's best to start praying.
I was looking for an easy fix that left me
straying.

At times I had failed to acknowledge that God's
love is sufficient.
For I was chasing a love story that was at best
inefficient.
Eventually I prayed the Lord would deliver me
from these soul ties.
I needed to understand that I was feeding my
soul lies.
I thought that I could buy love and friendship.
I feel shame to think of how I neglected Jesus
and I's relationship.

All that was left were empty promises.
All I knew is that I didn't need this.
That's what infatuation has to give.
This is not how I am to live...
Walking around as if I have no hope.
I was at the end of my rope.
God offers a love I do not deserve.
So with my life I will endlessly serve.

For I was addicted to an attention that couldn't
be sustained.
When I surrendered my kinship to God, I felt a
relief that can hardly be explained.
Thank You for Your grace Lord, for I truly
needed it.
I'm sorry I coveted a friendship when I should
have heeded it.
We were unevenly yoked but I wanted to feed
my flesh.
Jesus, thank you for your blood on Calvary that
upon repentance makes me fresh!

Dark Denim

There are things I fail to speak of.
I don't want the world to see all that I'm made of.
There are sins I have darker than thunderous
skies.
I long for the Father so I seek Him most times.
I'm sorry for the wrong things I've done
Especially when I became undone.

I listen and wait for I know there's a value to
stillness.
I contain my patience and I appreciate God's
gentleness.
At times nothing stifles silence more than tears
of regret.
At times nothing breaks the psyche more than
trauma you can't forget.
The grief inside, I wear it well.
High rise of emotions make my heart swell.

I fight my flesh to do what I believe is right.
Most days it doesn't seem so black and white.
Things run together and I don't always see
clearly .
I'm always running and sometimes I get weary.

Lord, hydrate me with Your Word and nourish
me with wisdom.
I'm not quitting this race nor will I give in and
lose momentum.
But I tread lightly as not to move in haste.
I will trust the Lord's timing and pace.

Dear Lord, please teach me your ways and then
some.
Enemies, I have chosen to forgive them.
When I lose the words, let me search Your
scripture.
When tears make it hard to see, let me trust You
know the bigger picture.
I've been drowning for so long.
God has had me all along.
I can put away my own agenda.
So I can stand in awe of Your splendor.

Best of Breathing

Laying in my hospital bed,
I adjusted the oxygen mask upon my head.
Struggling to breathe with pneumonia from
COVID-19,
I prayed that God would give my body strength to
keep fighting.
He is powerful and mighty so I knew He could
answer my prayers.
Although my prognosis was not promising, I felt
God's presence there.
Including in the ICU, all hooked up.
Every time I opened my eyes from a nap, I sent
praises up.

I remember coming home with oxygen,
wondering if I would breath independently again.
No smell for a year.
More faith and less fear.
Hard to keep food down and stand on my feet.
Suffering from rapid heartbeat.
God heard the pleas of my friends and family.
The Lord truly sustained me.
Thank you Father for not forsaking me.
Thank you God for healing me.

I was a goner from what the hospital originally told
me.
The Lord had a plan that I couldn't see.
When the survivor guilt attempts to rob me of my
joyfulness,
I remember to rejoice about God's faithfulness.

Lord, You are the Great Physician.
You can heal me in any position.
You can make me whole again.
Lord, You are my medicine.
Spoon-feed me scripture.
Help me see the bigger picture.

Make Your ways and my wrongs known.
Give me a peace that defeats feeling alone.
Wash me of anxiety.
God, You are my only deity.
There is no room for secular obsession.
My body is a temple of your possession.

Black Olive

Dear Lord, send me a sign.
I am Your olive from the vine.
Please tell me the olive don't fall far from the
tree.
I want to be more of You and less of me.
Let Your lessons rain on me.
Saturate the roots of my tree.
Help me grow from the dirt, moss and sand.
Help me draw closer to the Great I am.

Hope Fully

How do you describe the indescribable?
How do you explain the unexplainable?

How do you define that which is indefinite?
Our hope is infinite.

Our time is miniscule.
Trust God and let Him rule!

Lukewarm

Dear Lord, I don't want to be lukewarm.
I want to be like a palm tree in the storm.
With Your Holy Spirit in my heart,
I want to persevere, not fall apart.
Please give me the supernatural strength for trials that taunt me.
Please assist me with my armor to fight the enemy.

Dear Lord, I don't want to be lukewarm.
I do not want to summon the wrath of which You warn.
I want the discernment from the Holy Spirit.
I want a repentant heart instead of rationalizing it.

Dear Lord, I don't want to be lukewarm.
I give You my heart to transform.
I don't want to be spewed from Your mouth as You describe!
Jesus, I want You as my Bride!

Wandering Wide

I am one of Your sheep.
But I am tired in the field on my feet.

You call me to come so that You can give me
rest.
I am moving in Your peace though I am tired of
this test.

With You I can see greener pastures.
With You there's a promise of an ever after.

For even after my body is done working to the
bone,
You promise that I will never be alone.

When I wander, I hide even farther.
But you still search for me, my Faithful Father.

Hope, Hang-ups and Showers of Shamelessness

I once felt lifeless and without hope.
He breathed new life into me and I awoke.

After that, I could not remain the same.
How could I when Jesus took away all my
blame?

By His blood I am shameless.
By His blood I am blameless.

There's no telling what in the future I must
endure.
However, of this one thing I can be sure:

No sin is too great that He can't erase.
We gain wisdom when we search for His face.

I am seeking earnestly.
I am loving honestly.

I don't have to live in shame.
For there is power in His name!

I strive to meditate on His Word daily.
His Living Word sustains me.

I will pick up my cross each day.
I will sing praises to the Great Yahweh!

Entangled Engagement

I kept the ring.
I remember almost everything.
As if it were yesterday.
Sometimes I wonder if I made a mistake.
But an unevenly yoked marriage wouldn't be
blessed.
Ending the engagement made me hard-pressed.
That January afternoon he got down on one
knee.
He played a video he made and asked, "will you
marry me?"
I said yes and he put that ring upon my finger.
All that followed after is pain that would linger.

We started planning the wedding events and all
the fixings.
But what's a marriage without God's blessings?
I knew I should have said no.
I knew I was wrong from the get-go.
I wanted my Heavenly Father to approve.
I wanted the Holy Spirit's discernment to move.
I hoped my fiancé would accept Christ as his
Savior.
However, I didn't want him to become a
Christian to earn my favor.

Was I over-analyzing our engagement?
I was terrified of facing the embarrassment.
That's when the Lord came in and saved the day.
He redirected my attention and took my guilt
away.
I wanted to follow the Word no mater how bad it
hurt.
I knew that I couldn't make our engagement
work.

Sometimes doing the right thing could involve
breaking a heart.
Sometimes God moves two lovers to part.
This doesn't mean He don't love us.
It doesn't mean there's no one for us.
God has ordered our steps indeed.
We need to increase our faith and let Him lead.

I cancelled the bride subscriptions and my train
ticket.
I hope some day my ex-fiancé understands why
I did it.
I hope the example I gave planted a spiritual
seed.
I pray that someday his family forgives me.
Sometimes we rush into things when we should
be still.

He told me to keep the ring, which I did and
probably always will.
It took over a year to delete my wedding
playlist.
It has taken me awhile for my heart to adjust.

It's important to grow through what you're going
through.
To trust that God knows what's best for you.
Thank you God for teaching me this lesson.
Help me not to miss Your blessing.
Sometimes a love that comes so fast,
doesn't have enough roots to last.

From Fixed on Food to Fixed on God

Contemplating every bite.
Fighting all my cellulite.

I don't desire to be a glutton.
Is my hunger masking something?

Dear Lord, please help me break through this
addiction with food.
Please give me a smile through every mood.

So much You have done for me.
Help me lift my cross daily.

Gingerbread Girl

When I was younger, I didn't want to be brown.
It was a hue that was not appreciated in that
small town.

There were years I was mad at God for making
me this way.
Now I trust His Word that I am fearfully and
wonderfully made.

I learned self-loathing as a student in elementary.
God took away my concern of what people think
about me.

Although bullying at times breaks my heart,
I remind myself how the Bible says Christians
are set apart.

For years I let low self-esteem get the best of
me.
Until I rediscovered in Christ my identity.

I'm truly ready for God to be the Author of my
life story.
I sincerely trust He wants the best for me.

Life got better when I forgave.
I've prayed for my enemies and turned the page.

Childhood wounds are now behind me.
Turning the other cheek has blessed me
abundantly.

Sure Things

God loves me indeed.
All He asks is that I plant a seed.

For what I sow I will reap.
There's not one promise He won't keep.

I can't be sure in my life of many things.
But I can be sure of these things:

God is amazing and He is true.
God, I know this life is not about me but about
You.

Sometimes I toss and turn from when I've lucid
dreamed.
Falsities of love and friendship through God can
be redeemed.

Even if all my friends can only be counted on
one hand,
at least with Christ I know where His love does
stand.

His Love waits when I slide back.
His Love is ready to guide me back on track.

Every time I've felt myself slip away from the
truth,
His Love never stopped following through.

Don't be afraid to wait - sometimes that's the
only way.
To wait on the Lord with our hearts and minds
ready to pray.

Don't be afraid to show your heart to the Father.
There's no One who will love you harder.

Jesus is the only carpenter you need.
All He asks for compensation is the faith of a
mustard seed.

Jesus has the tools to rebuild what's broken
inside.
His love is the catalyst of which I long to abide.

Flesh Wars

Satisfaction has become my distraction.
Instant gratification...
A luxurious vacation.
Concerts galore.
But what about what God has in store?
I've been missing the point for so long.
I can't hear over this lustful song.
I get on and off the bandwagon.
I want to follow Him and then I stop again.
I have been redeemed and am determined to
commit.
So much Jesus done and I take Communion to
not forget.

Addictive Appetites and Apprehensiveness

Lust, why are you hard to give up?
Jesus, You look beyond my sin to my inner
crust.

You found something in me worth saving.
So why is it hard for me to give up this craving?

What You've done, I can never repay.
Holy One, please help me day-by-day.

I need Your strength to endure this race.
Good Shepherd, thank You for not leaving even
though this lamb has a slow pace.

I know love is not found in a bar or necessarily
on dating sites.
Lord, You are the Only One that deserves my
days and nights.

Fishing for compliments that fall between the
cracks of my every void.
Your Word confirms that You give us the
strength to fight temptations we must avoid.

Why do I long for a human to wrap their arms
around my waist?
For these bring happy feelings that eventually
fade.

But the joy of the Lord is everlasting.
It breaks through any pain I am masking!

Vast Love

God's love is vast.
It's bigger than my dirty past.

God's love is a big wave.
So big He sent His son to conquer the grave.

God's love is bigger than I can imagine.
So much it covers a multitude of sin.

God's love is massive.
So large that He can get me past this.

God's love is huge.
So grand that He is my refuge.

God's love is a giant arsenal.
So protective that He wants our relationship
personal.

God's love is unconditional.
So much so that He gives me strength to conquer
battles that are spiritual.

God's love is merciful.
So much that I can always be hopeful.

God's love is healing.
That's why I know I can fight this depressive
feeling.

God's love sets me free.
In His love is where I long to be.

If ever I feel my faith begin to falter,
I pray for the willingness to leave my burdens at
the alter.

For God's love is so giant that He sent His Son
for sins to be paid.
Thank You Lord that we are fearfully and
wonderfully made.

God's love is ever-flowing.
So seamlessly that no matter what, I can keep on
growing.

God's love is so beautiful.
To the point that He grants us grace when we are
sinful.

God loves us beyond our own comprehension.
God's love for us has no beginning or ending.